Hajj Harmonies: Nursery Rhymes Colouring Book

Elizabeth Lymer (text; design)
Kim Reimann (illustrations; design)
Sandy Quigley (illustrations)

Mindworks Publishing
Copyright © 2014 by Elizabeth Lymer and Mindworks Publishing

Published by Mindworks Publishing,
Missouri City, TX 77489

mindworkspublishing@gmail.com

Hajj Harmonies videos can be streamed free of charge and without advertisements via the 'Elizabeth Lymer' YouTube channel at http://www.youtube.com.

Hajj Harmonies

Nursery Rhymes Colouring Book

Hajj Harmonies
Nursery Rhymes Colouring Book

By Elizabeth Lymer (text; design), Kim Reimann (illustrations; design), and Sandy Quigley (illustrations)

Order of Nursery Rhymes

Hajj Is The Great Pilgrimage (Mary Had A Little Lamb)

A Long, Full Coach (A Big Red Bus)

Peace, Pilgrims, Young (Pease Porridge Hot)

Round The Ka'bah, Walk (Wind The Bobbin Up)

Peace Greetings Must Be Spread (Good Morning Mrs Hen)

Umm Isma'il (Jack And Jill)

There's Plenty Of Shelter (There Was An Old Woman Who Lived In A Shoe)

Up The Mountain (Jack Be Nimble)

Throw Your Pebbles (Humpty Dumpty)

'Eid For Everybody (Sing A Song Of Sixpence)

The Sacrifice Is For Allah Alone (The Big Ship Sails On The Ally-Ally-Oh)

Two Muslim Pilgrims (Two Little Dickie Birds)

Hajj Is The Great Pilgrimage

(Mary Had A Little Lamb)

Hajj is the great pilgrimage
Which we Muslims make,
Leaving all our daily cares,
We go for Allah's sake.

All wear very simple dress
And round the Ka'bah go,
Praising Allah – He's the best,
We point to the black stone.

From Safa we rush to Marwah,
At Arafat we stand,
At Mina stand at the Jamrah
And throw pebbles by hand.

Hajj Is The Great Pilgrimage

(Continued)

At Al-Masjid-al-Haram
We all make special prayer,
Drink the water from Zamzam,
On 'Eid day we cut hair.

And on Hajj, when it is 'Eid,
We sacrifice that day,
Share the meat with those in need,
And feast in our own way.

More Muslims make Hajj every year,
You may well want to know –
Why *do* Muslims hold Hajj so dear?
You'll find out if you go!

A Long, Full Coach

(A Big Red Bus)

A long, full coach,

A long, full coach,

A crowded mini bus,

And a long, full coach.

A long, full coach,

A long, full coach,

A crowded mini bus,

And a long, full coach.

A Long, Full Coach

(Continued)

A train ride, a train ride,
A crowded mini bus,
And a long, full coach.

A train ride, a train ride,
A crowded mini bus,
And a long, full coach.

Travel, travel, let's make Hajj to please Allah!
Travel, travel, let's make Hajj to please Allah!

Peace, Pilgrims, Young

(Pease Pudding Hot)

Peace, pilgrims, young,

Peace, pilgrims, old,

Peace, pilgrims making Hajj,

As we're told.

Some make Hajj young,

Some make Hajj old,

All able Muslims must,

As we're told.

Round The Ka'bah, Walk

(Wind The Bobbin Up)

Round the Ka'bah, walk,
Round the Ka'bah, walk,
Boys, girls, men and women.

Round the Ka'bah, one,
Round the Ka'bah, two,
Three, four, five, six, seven.

Point to the black stone,
As you walk by,
Touch it or kiss it,
If you're close-by.

Say, Allah's the Greatest,
Once, twice, thrice,
Name and praise Him,
Be precise.

Peace Greetings Must Be Spread

(Good Morning Mrs Hen)

Peace, peace, peace, peace, peace;

Peace greetings must be spread.

How do we spread the peace about?

Listen, here's what's said:

Assalaam 'alaykum,

The peace be upon you,

Wa 'alaykum as-salaam,

And peace be upon you.

Peace, peace, peace, peace, peace;

And mercy can be spread.

How do we spread the mercy too?

Listen, here's what's said:

Wa rahmatullahi

Wa rahmatullah,

We can all spread Allah's peace

And mercy of Allah!

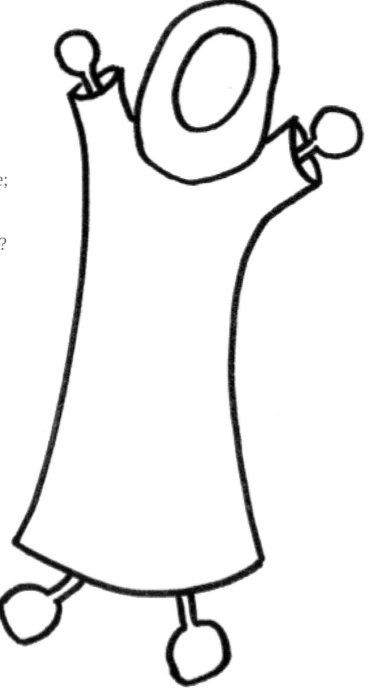

Peace Greetings Must Be Spread

(Continued)

Peace, peace, peace, peace, peace;

And blessings can be spread.

How do we spread the blessings too?

Listen, here's what's said:

Say, wa barakaatuh,

Wa barakaatuhu,

We can all spread Allah's peace,

Mercy and blessings too!

Umm Isma'il

(Jack And Jill)

Umm Isma'il went up the hill
To find her son some water,
She looked around from on high ground,
From Safa she went up Marwah.

When she had been sev'n times between,
And all this time found nothing,
Allah Most Kind to humankind
Provided her with a new spring!

There's Plenty Of Shelter

(There Was An Old Woman Who Lived In A Shoe)

There's plenty of shelter for pilgrims to use,

There are so many tents you mayn't know whose is whose,

They all look the same, their colour is white –

The tents up at Mina to sleep in at night.

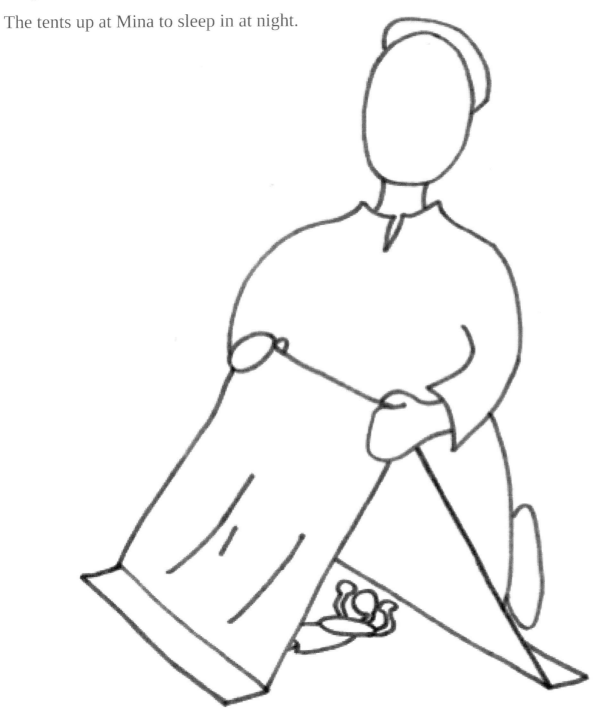

Up The Mountain

(Jack Be Nimble)

Up the mountain,
Down the plain,
Pray for mercy
And pray again.

On the mountain,
On the flat,
Pray for mercy
At Arafat.

Throw Your Pebbles

(Humpty Dumpty)

Throw your pebbles straight at the wall,

Stone the Devil – don't heed his call,

Ibrahim firmly three times told him no,

So throw your pebbles, tell Shaytan to go!

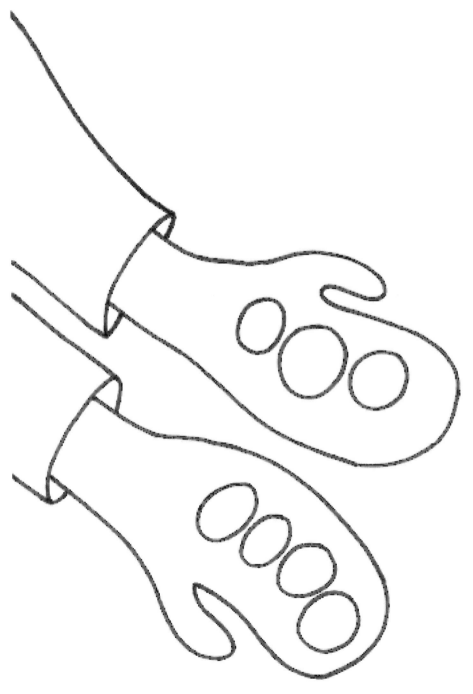

'Eid For Everybody

(Sing A Song Of Sixpence)

'Eid for everybody,

A festival today,

Muslims round the whole world

Read, pray and say:

Allah is the greatest,

There is no god but He,

And Allah is the one to praise.

To Him belongs glory.

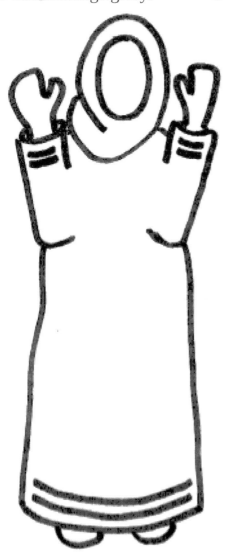

'Eid For Everybody

(Continued)

The women get dressed in clean clothes,

With clean teeth and bodies,

The men all get dressed in clean clothes,

With clean teeth and bodies.

The children also dress up,

Often in new clothes,

And go along for 'Eid Salah,

And pray in the rows.

The Sacrifice Is For Allah Alone

(The Big Ship Sails On The Ally-Ally-Oh)

The sacrifice is for Allah alone, Allah alone, Allah alone.

Oh, the sacrifice is for Allah alone, on the day of 'Eid-ul-Adha.

Ibrahim was a prophet of Allah, prophet of Allah, prophet of Allah.

Oh, Ibrahim was a prophet of Allah, and he was a father.

Allah told him to sacrifice his son, sacrifice his son, sacrifice his son.

Oh, Allah told him to sacrifice his son, and he obeyed his Master.

Shaytan told him to disobey Allah, disobey Allah, disobey Allah,

Oh, Shaytan told him to disobey Allah, but he obeyed his Master.

Allah was pleased and asked for a ram instead, for a ram instead, for a ram instead.

Oh, Allah was pleased and asked for a ram instead, Most Merciful Creator.

The sacrifice is for Allah alone, Allah alone, Allah alone.

Oh, the sacrifice is for Allah alone, on the day of 'Eid-ul-Adha.

Two Muslim Pilgrims

(Two Little Dickie Birds)

Two Muslim pilgrims are

Sitting on a train;

One named Zainab,

One named Zain.

Go on Hajj Zainab!

Go on Hajj Zain!

Come back Zainab!

Come back Zain!

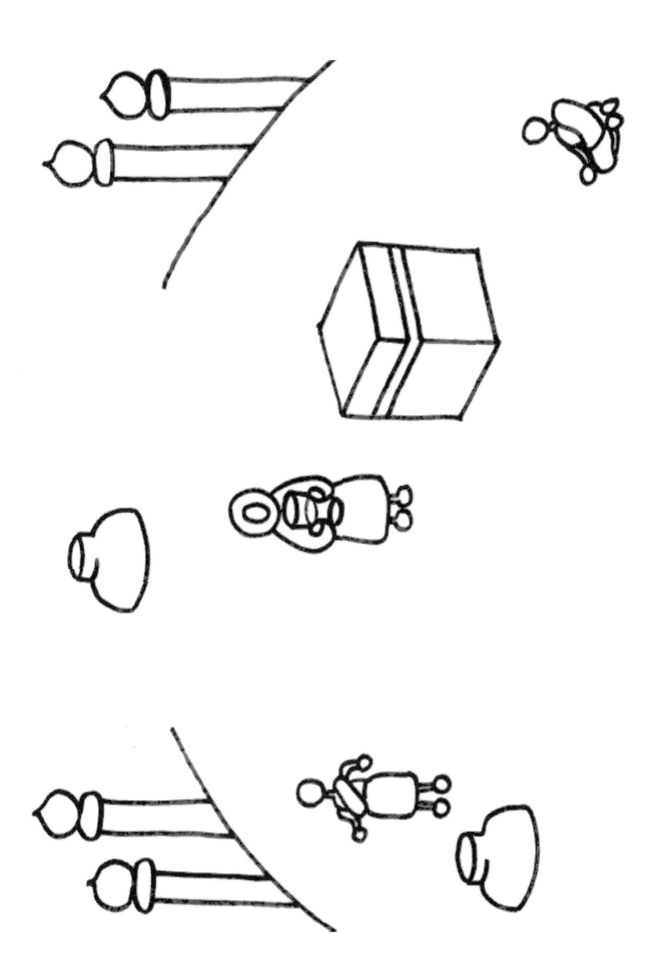

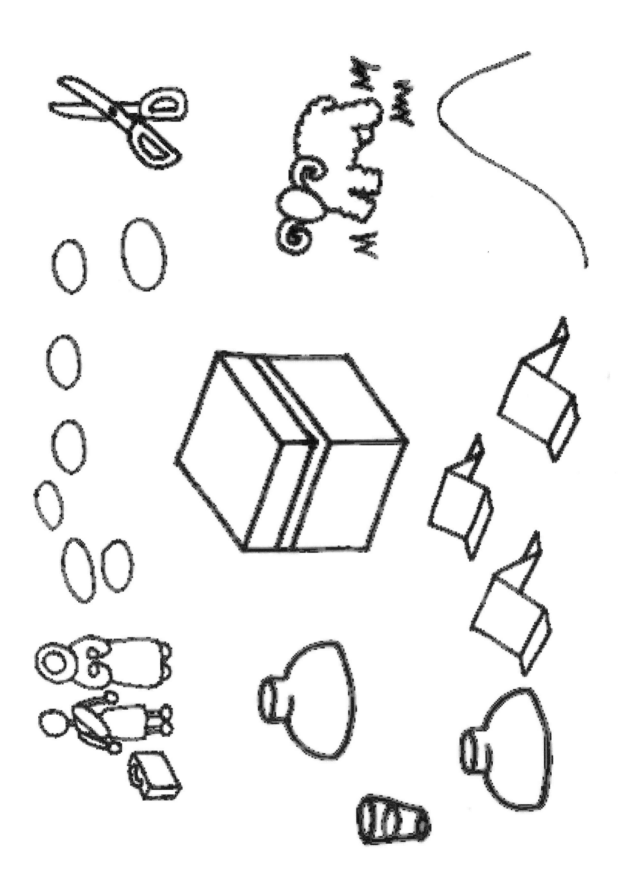

Made in the USA
Middletown, DE
06 February 2016